J
363.73
Kee

6240402
14.95

Keeping the air clean

KEEPING THE
AIR CLEAN

Text: Rosa Costa-Pau
Illustrations: Estudio Marcel Socías

El Cuidado del Aire © Copyright Parramón
Ediciones, S. A. Published by Parramón
Ediciones, S. A., Barcelona, Spain.

1 3 5 7 9 8 6 4 2

Cuidado del aire. English.
  Keeping the air clean.
    p. cm.—(The Junior library of ecology.)
  Translation of: El Cuidado del aire.
  Includes index.
  ISBN 0-7910-2103-3
  1. Air quality management—Juvenile
literature. 2. Air—Pollution—Juvenile
literature. [1. Air—Pollution. 2. Pollution.] I.
Chelsea House Publishers. II. Title. III. Series.
TD883.13.C8513 1994   93-19881
363.73'92—dc20   CIP
                                          AC

Contents

The Junior Library of Ecology

KEEPING THE AIR CLEAN

CHELSEA HOUSE PUBLISHERS

New York • Philadelphia

The Earth's Atmosphere

An Enormous Layer of Air

The earth is surrounded by a layer of air called the atmosphere. The atmosphere can be compared to the skin of an orange, but with one important difference. The edge of an orange's skin is perfectly defined, whereas the air around our planet becomes thinner the higher up you go until—at about 250 miles above the surface of the earth—it practically disappears.

The Workings of the Atmosphere

The earth has an atmosphere because of the force of gravity, which keeps it in position. If there were no gravity, atmospheric gases would simply float into outer space.

If the atmosphere did not exist, the sky would not be blue; it would be black and blanketed in stars—even during the day. Sunlight would roast our planet.

There are continents, seas, rivers, and lakes on our planet. Above these, there is a gaseous layer made up of the air we breathe.

▼

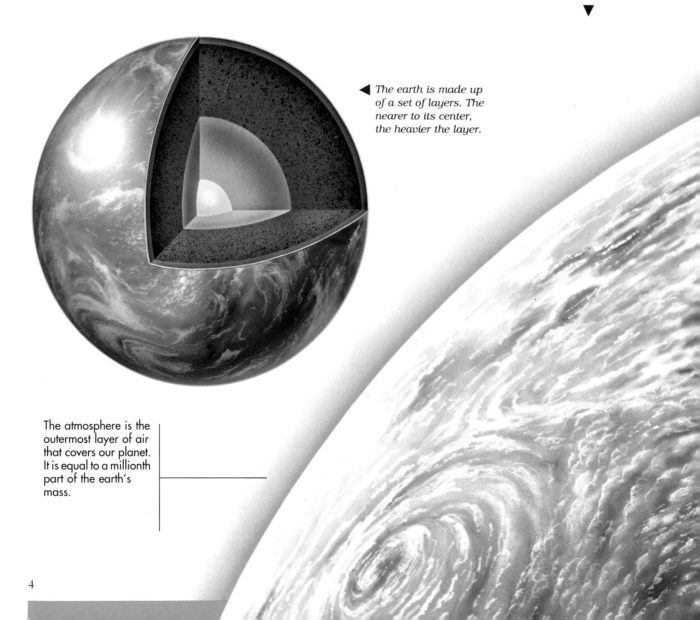

◀ *The earth is made up of a set of layers. The nearer to its center, the heavier the layer.*

The atmosphere is the outermost layer of air that covers our planet. It is equal to a millionth part of the earth's mass.

Without our atmosphere there would be no rain. There would only be constant meteor showers. There would be no dawn or dusk. Without our atmosphere there would be no life on earth.

Besides acting as a protective shield, the atmosphere generates many meteorological phenomena such as storms, hurricanes, lightning, and torrential rains, which, aside from their destructive elements, are symptoms of the constant changes taking place in our atmosphere.

Air Pollution

Forest fires, industrial smoke, emissions produced by the burning of oil, coal, or natural gas, are all consequences of human activities. They can produce changes in the atmosphere and reduce its capacity to protect life on earth.

The atmosphere protects the earth. There are also such phenomena as wind and clouds, which along with other factors influence the earth's climate.

The Composition of the Atmosphere

The Gases in the Air

Toward the end of the 18th century, the French chemist Lavoisier proved that air was a chemical composite. He demonstrated this by separating it into two gases. One gas made the flame he had applied to it brighter. It was also breathable. He called this gas oxygen. The flame did not burn in the other gas, and it was not breathable either. He called this gas nitrogen.

Today, however, we know that the composition of air is much more complex and the proportion of gases that form it are not always uniform.

Dust and Liquid Particles in the Atmosphere

Apart from the gaseous components and water vapor, there are also suspended solid particles in the atmosphere. They come from different sources—some are dust particles that originated from soil erosion; others come from volcanic eruptions and forest fires; some particles are even the remains of meteorites. There are also liquid particles present in the atmosphere. They are known as aerosols. They are formed from sea evaporation and are also called marine aerosols.

Marine aerosols form when the air strikes the sea's surface and produces waves. Small bubbles are produced that release liquid particles, which are picked up and carried by the wind.

These particles also contain organic wastes originating from decomposed algae and plankton, as well as chemical elements, the most abundant of them being common salt, or sodium chloride.

The marine aerosols act as a kind of delivery vehicle for chemical substances to other regions of the earth, where they are deposited on the ground.

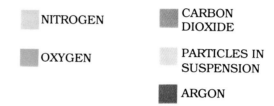

NITROGEN

OXYGEN

CARBON DIOXIDE

PARTICLES IN SUSPENSION

ARGON

THE COMPONENTS OF THE AIR:

Nitrogen
is the most abundant element in the atmosphere, making up almost 80% of atmospheric gases.

Oxygen
is indispensable for breathing.

Carbon dioxide
is necessary for plant life, because plants use it to carry out photosynthesis.

Argon
and other inert gases are present in minute quantities.

Particles in suspension
are found in different amounts and combinations, including dust particles, pollen spores, and an ever-increasing quantity of pollutants.

Water vapor
is also present. The quantity of water vapor depends on the amount of clouds and rainfall.

Marine aerosols and dust particles are necessary for water vapor condensation. If they did not exist, water vapor would have nothing to condense around, and rain and precipitation would be much rarer.

The solid particles released during a volcanic eruption become incorporated into the air.

Sea evaporation fills the atmosphere with liquid particles.

Forest fires and soil erosion increase the amount of dust particles in the air.

The Different Layers of Air

Depending on the height, air undergoes changes in the proportions of its components, in the concentration of its particles—that is, in its density—and above all in its temperature. These variations make it possible to distinguish different layers of the atmosphere.

The Lower Layers

The lowest layer, which is in contact with the earth's surface, is called the troposphere. This is where air masses circulate and where meterological phenomena occur, as well as where all living organisms interact with the atmosphere through respiration and photosynthesis. In the 6-mile-deep troposphere, the higher you go, the lower the temperature.

The next layer is the stratosphere, which goes up to a height of about 50 miles above the surface. Here, the higher up you go, the hotter it is. Because of this increase in temperature, a significant amount of oxygen is not found in a normal molecular state—that is, in molecules consisting of two oxygen atoms—but in molecules of three atoms. The oxygen in this layer is called ozone. It has a very important role of keeping out harmful ultraviolet radiation emitted by the sun. Some ozone molecules decompose and form normal oxygen. We call this part of the stratosphere the ozone layer.

The Highest Layers of the Atmosphere

Between 50 and 375 miles above the surface the ionosphere is found, and on top of that the exosphere gradually merges with the vacuum of interstellar space.

Where Does the Atmosphere End?

Density, that is, the concentration of particles, thins out with height. At a certain height, there is total silence, because the distance between air particles is so great that they are incapable of carrying sound waves.

The division of the atmosphere into layers is only approximate because 95% of the air's total mass is concentrated in the first 8 miles. We still cannot precisely define where the last layer of the atmosphere is and where cosmic space begins.

In the lower regions of the atmosphere, the ▶ *temperature decreases with height and soon reaches sub-zero temperatures. At 30 miles above the surface, the temperature begins to increase. A little farther up, still in the stratosphere, it begins to decrease once again, until it reaches 250° F below zero. In the ionosphere, at 50 to 60 miles above the earth's surface, the temperature quickly rises until it reaches very high levels.*

300 miles
(+6300° F)

250 miles
(+4500° F)

190 miles
(+2700° F)

125 miles
(+1500° F)

60 miles
(+600° F)

50 miles
(–180° F)

30 miles
(+70° F)

6 miles
(–76° F)

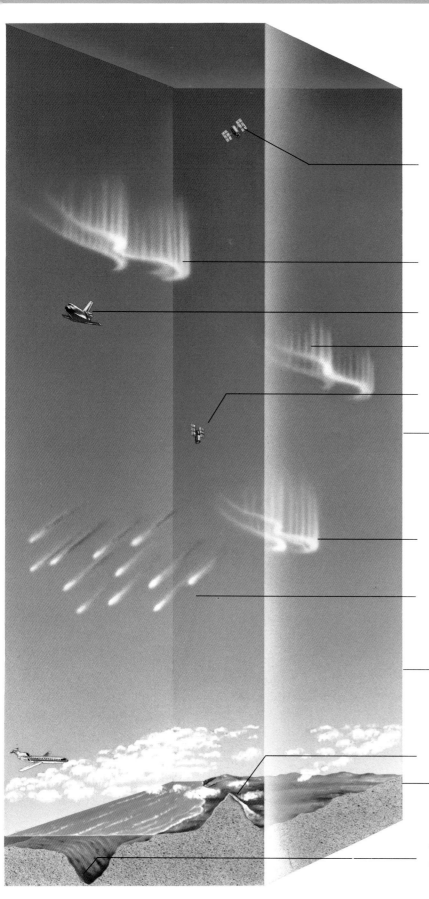

EXOSPHERE

SPACE SATELLITES

AURORA BOREALIS

SPACE SHUTTLE

AURORA BOREALIS

METEOROLOGICAL SATELLITES

The zone farthest from the earth's surface. It begins at about 375 miles above the surface and ends at an undetermined height, where space begins. Air molecules are very rare—they can be separated from one another by up to 60 miles. The lightest gases escape the earth's gravitational pull and disperse into space.

IONOSPHERE

AURORA BOREALIS

METEORS

It ranges from 60 to 375 miles above the earth. Its name originates from the abundance of ions (electrically charged particles) found in this layer. Many meteorites disintegrate in this layer when they enter the atmosphere from space. They can be seen in the night skies and are called shooting stars.

STRATOSPHERE

MT. EVEREST
(27,000 feet)

It reaches 60 miles above the earth. It is a zone where there is abundant ozone, which prevents some solar radiation from reaching the earth.

TROPOSPHERE

OCEAN TRENCH
(30,000 feet deep)

It is 6 miles thick and is the layer that is directly in contact with the earth's surface. The troposphere is where meterological phenomena take place.

The Sun's Radiation

A Filter and Protective Layer

If it were not for the atmosphere, life on earth would not be possible. The atmosphere is like a filter that allows through only the electromagnetic radiation that sustains or is not harmful to developing life.

An herbivore in search of grass needs the solar energy that is stored in plant cells. The herbivore converts it into useful energy for motion, metabolism, and other needs.

Types of Solar Radiation

After traveling 93 million miles through space, solar energy reaches the earth in the form of electromagnetic waves. These waves have different names according to their wave length and frequency: gamma rays, X rays, ultraviolet waves, infra-red rays, and radio waves.

Negative and Positive Effects

Short wave radiation, such as ultraviolet light, carries a lot of energy and can damage living organisms. The ozone absorbs much of this harmful radiation.

Longer waves, such as infrared rays, do not carry much energy and their effect at the surface of the earth is only to increase the temperature.

Light waves can be used by certain molecules in plant matter, such as chlorophyll. Chlorophyll performs the process of photosynthesis, which produces food for plants and eventually food for herbivores.

Green plants transform solar energy into chemical energy stored in food substances, providing herbivores with the necessary energy to survive. When going from one form of energy to another, the energy degrades. Some of it is transformed into heat and escapes into the atmosphere.

▼

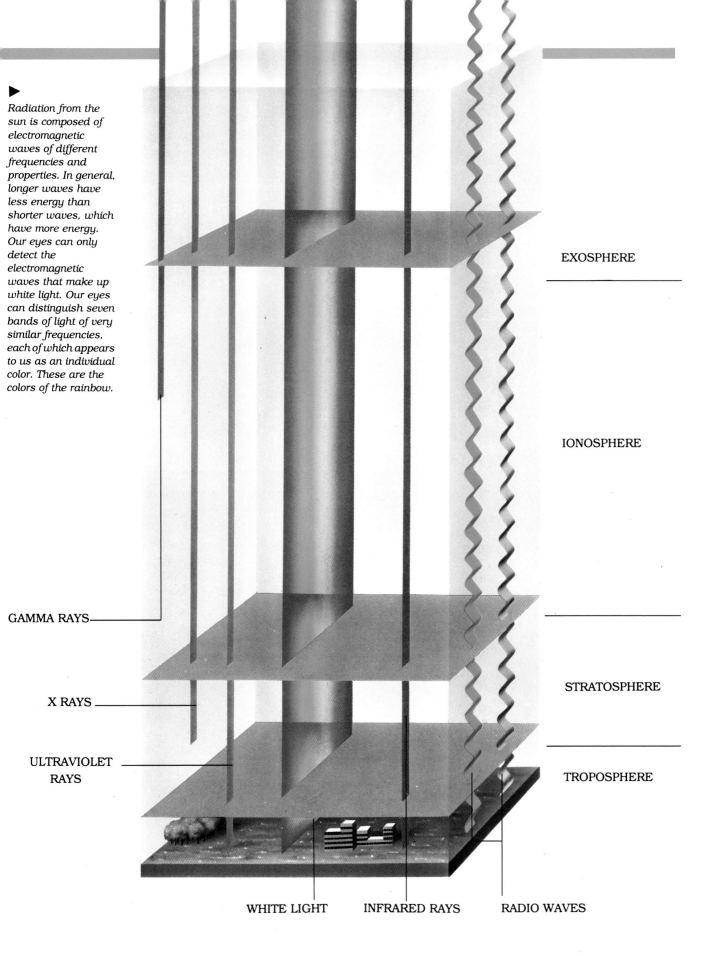

▶ *Radiation from the sun is composed of electromagnetic waves of different frequencies and properties. In general, longer waves have less energy than shorter waves, which have more energy. Our eyes can only detect the electromagnetic waves that make up white light. Our eyes can distinguish seven bands of light of very similar frequencies, each of which appears to us as an individual color. These are the colors of the rainbow.*

EXOSPHERE

IONOSPHERE

GAMMA RAYS

STRATOSPHERE

X RAYS

ULTRAVIOLET RAYS

TROPOSPHERE

WHITE LIGHT   INFRARED RAYS   RADIO WAVES

Energy Transfers

The Balance Between Heat and Energy

Just like other bodies in our solar system, the earth possesses an energy equilibrium, that is, it radiates as much energy into space as it receives from the sun. If this did not happen, the world would have excessively cooled down or heated up by now.

This balance is maintained by our atmosphere, which prevents the heat stored on the ground from radiating too quickly into space. The atmosphere also stops dangerous levels of solar radiation from reaching the surface.

The radiation that does reach the earth's surface is transformed into heat. This heat produces variations in the earth's temperature as well as in the masses of air that are in contact with the earth's surface. This process determines, to a certain extent, the climates of the different regions of the earth.

So the atmosphere carries out an important job in redistributing solar energy all over the world, and from there into space again.

Human Activity

There have always been solid particles in the atmosphere, originating from volcanic eruptions, soil erosion, and so on. The substances generated by such events can be considered to be potential pollutants. But nature is perfectly capable of taking care of this kind of pollution, thanks to the atmosphere's ability to purify itself.

However, the balance among that atmosphere's component elements is very fragile. If man adds his own pollutants, the balance may alter dramatically.

The greatest danger comes from human activities that have a direct effect on the atmosphere. Until recently man has treated the atmosphere like an enormous natural rubbish dump. Industrial waste has been released into the atmosphere without considering what effects it might produce.

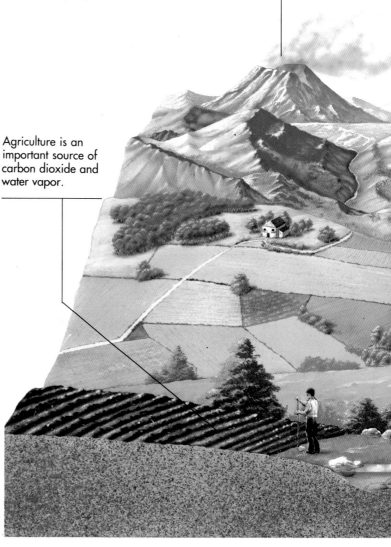

Volcanos release large quantities of carbon dioxide and solid particles.

Agriculture is an important source of carbon dioxide and water vapor.

Heat and energy originate from the solar radiation that penetrates the atmosphere. The radiation that doesn't reach the earth is absorbed or reflected back into space by the earth's atmosphere. Visible light and radio waves are the types of radiation that reach the earth. The types of radiation that are absorbed by the atmosphere or are reflected back into space are gamma rays and X rays.

The gases in the atmosphere act as regulators of the sun's energy and the heat produced on the surface. Some gases are found in many processes related to life on earth. ▼

Livestock contribute to the levels of carbon dioxide and water vapor in the atmosphere by way of respiration.

Acid Rain

Oxides Turn into Acids

The chemicals sulfur dioxide and various nitrogen oxides are very abundant in industrial smoke.

These components are released into the atmosphere where they are subjected to various physical processes and chemical transformations. The most important chemical reaction is the transformation of these oxides into acids. Sulfuric acid and nitric acid incorporate themselves into rain drops in the troposphere, causing a change in their chemical composition. When this takes place we call it acid rain.

Different Degrees of Acid

The pH scale is used to indicate the presence of acid in substances. Distilled water is neutral; it doesn't contain acid. Rainwater, however, always has a small quantity of acid. When rainwater has a pH level of less than 5, it is considered to be acid rain. This means that it contains an excessive amount of acid molecules dissolved within it.

The Effects of Acid Rain

Contaminated rainwater transports acid, subjecting lakes, rivers, oceans, forests and fields, and towns and cities to its effects.

The acidification of lakes and rivers mainly affects the fish, which are the most sensitive species to any change in the pH levels of their environment. It becomes increasingly more difficult for them to breathe, and they finally die.

The most serious consequences of acid rain are in the land's ecosystems. Acid rain depletes the nutrients in the soil and alters the number of microorganisms. This has repercussions on the development of plant life.

Acid rain is caused by a chemical reaction in certain substances such as sulfur oxides and nitrogen oxides. These substances originate from power stations, factory smoke stacks, and car exhausts. The pollutants are then incorporated into the clouds and fall back to earth in the form of rain and snow, destroying forests.

A NORMAL LAKE AND FOREST

A POLLUTED LAKE AND FOREST

Ground and Atmospheric Acids

Vegetation not only is affected by the acidification of the soil but also by the acid rain itself. Vegetation loses its ability to protect itself from the cold of winter and the dryness of summer, as well as from plant diseases.

Sometimes trees shed their leaves in an attempt to free themselves of the pollutants. They then produce new shoots in their place. They are what we might call emergency shoots.

The Pollutant Cycle

Natural Cycles

Chemical substances are constantly passing from one organism to another and between organisms and the environment. The way in which these substances move is called a cycle. A cycle is a constant circulation of an element such as carbon, oxygen, phosphorus, or nitrogen.

Certain transformations take place in the atmosphere and new substances are generated. For example, ozone become oxygen, nitrogen forms nitrogen oxides and later on becomes nitric acid.

Solar energy produces physical transformations in the atmosphere, such as the changes in the state of the water from vapor to liquid to ice. All this leads us to consider the earth and the atmosphere as a closed system made up of different cycles of solid, liquid, and gaseous substances.

The Changes in Cycles

Sulfur in the air originates from the combustion of gasoline, coal, and natural gas in industrial activities, and from the exhaust pipes of cars.

The sulfur molecules drift into high levels of the troposphere. There they become sulfur dioxide and later on sulfuric acid, which is picked up by rain drops and falls to the earth in the form of acid rain.

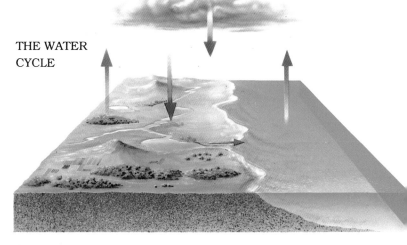

THE WATER CYCLE

▲

Water is constantly moving between and through plants and animals. It moves on the surface and underground, flowing to the sea. Seawater, river and lake water, as well as underground water, evaporate and condense in the clouds. Water then falls in the form of rain or snow. This is called the water cycle.

Once in the atmosphere, these oxides become acids.

Sulfur oxides and nitrogen oxides are emitted into the atmosphere by factories.

THE CARBON
CYCLE

▲
The living matter of all organisms is based on carbon. In the carbon cycle, this element enters the atmosphere from its sources on the land, travels by air currents, and then is absorbed by marine plankton and green plants that carry out photosynthesis.

Transporting Pollution

Clouds can travel very great distances, and in different directions, before they release their water. But the place where acid rain falls is not generally in the area where the sulfur was formed. It can fall in far-away areas, and the ecosystems there will suffer the effects of the pollutants. Because of the wind and the rain, there are cities that "export" their pollution to neighboring countries.

The effects of acid rain are often forgotten or ignored because they are found hundreds of miles away from the area where they are produced.

The acids are transported in clouds by the action of the wind.

Acidic snow or rain can fall hundreds and even thousands of miles from its place of origin.

◄
Sulfur dioxide is one of the most common forms of atmospheric pollution. It originates in the combustion of coal and oil used in energy production and readily enters the atmosphere. There it is transported by the wind to other regions.

The Greenhouse Effect

The Earth's Umbrella

Just like other bodies, the earth and its atmosphere emit energy in the form of heat. Heat energy radiated by the earth to the atmosphere, instead of dispersing into space, becomes trapped within the atmosphere, thanks to the effect of certain atmospheric gases. This is the greenhouse effect, in which the earth's surface and the lower regions of the atmosphere maintain sufficient levels of heat to sustain life.

The atmosphere contains certain gases that retain the heat given off by the planet. Some of these gases are carbon dioxide, nitrogen oxides, water vapor, and methane. They are all found in a natural state in the atmosphere. These are gases that produce the greenhouse effect.

Retaining Heat

The amount of these gases can increase because of human activity. This can be very dangerous, because if the atmosphere retains too much heat the earth will become too hot. The gradual overheating of the earth is called global warming.

Trees are the species that assimilate the most carbon dioxide, using it to create food and new plant tissue through photosynthesis. Trees act as "regulators" of this greenhouse gas.

Because of the gradual disappearance of forested areas that absorb carbon dioxide, the atmospheric quantity of this gas could be greatly increased in the future.

We must also take into account the effects of the combustion of oil, natural gas, and

► *The greenhouse effect is caused by the presence of gases such as carbon dioxide in the atmosphere, which absorbs a certain amount of solar radiation and heats the earth's surface, acting like the glass of a greenhouse that traps heat.*

Carbon monoxide, released by car exhaust pipes, is also a greenhouse gas.

The disappearance of forests around the world is one of the main causes of global warming.

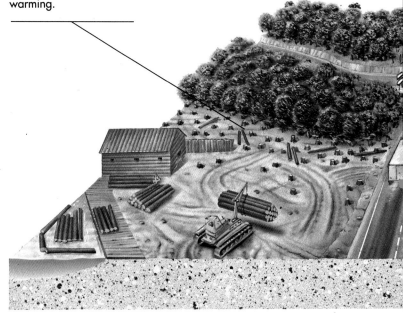

coal in industry. Twenty billion tons of carbon dioxide are released into the atmosphere every year, mostly as a result of industrial activity. Industrial processes increase the carbon dioxide content of the air and prevent the earth from discarding excess heat.

Global warming is also caused by gases called CFCs. Ultraviolet light frees the chlorine that is found in these gases. The chlorine then decomposes the particles of the ozone layer, reducing its concentration in the stratosphere. The result is that ultraviolet radiation can more easily penetrate the atmosphere.

Apart from dangerously increasing the temperature on the earth, ultraviolet radiation can damage plant tissues. Seeds and plankton might stop producing food.

Industrial emissions, human activities, ocean pollution that prevents the exchange of gases with the atmosphere, and the impoverishment of the soil due to modern agricultural techniques and intensive livestock rearing, are all factors that influence the changes that are taking place in the atmosphere, affecting the earth's climate. Intense volcanic activity can also produce climatic changes.

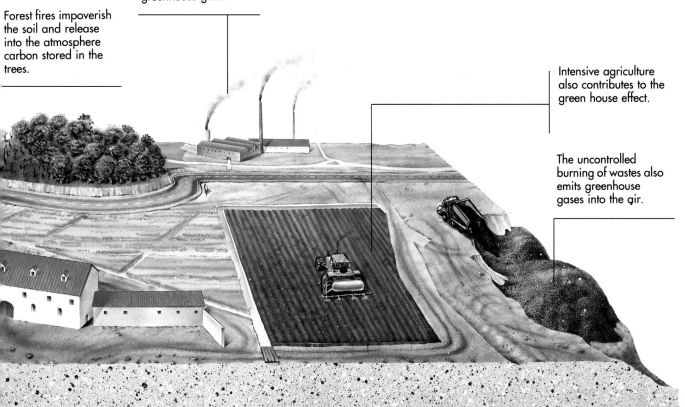

The smoke certain industries emit into the air contains greenhouse gases.

Forest fires impoverish the soil and release into the atmosphere carbon stored in the trees.

Intensive agriculture also contributes to the green house effect.

The uncontrolled burning of wastes also emits greenhouse gases into the air.

Atmospheric Ozone

The Long Life of Pollutants

Pollutants do not remain in the lower atmosphere for very long. Instead, they are transformed by chemical reactions that take place in the troposphere, or they return to the earth's surface.

Certain pollutants are dispersed in the air and reach the higher regions of the stratosphere. In this part of the atmosphere, air masses only move in a horizontal direction. For this reason, pollution can remain at this level for a long time, even hundreds of years.

The Ozone's Function

The most characteristic phenomenon of the stratosphere is the formation and transformation of ozone. Ozone is present in practically all atmospheric regions,

but the stratosphere is where ozone has its greatest effect on life on earth and on the atmosphere's dynamics. Ozone absorbs ultraviolet radiation from the sun. It performs a vital role in protecting life on our planet.

Ozone forms in equatorial regions, where solar radiation is most intense. A great part of this ozone is transferred in a horizontal direction by air masses to the earth's poles. The rest disperses and its concentration in various areas changes throughout the year.

Air currents can transport certain pollutants from a lower region of the atmosphere to the stratosphere, up to 60 miles above the earth's surface. These pollutants can remain in the stratosphere for a long time, perhaps for centuries before returning to earth.

▼

►
Ozone formation occurs most rapidly in the atmosphere above the equator. Much of it is transported by masses of air to the polar regions.

Stratospheric Ozone

Ultraviolet radiation striking the stratosphere can decompose ozone in the presence of certain chemicals. One of the most efficient ozone-destroying chemicals is chlorine.

The risk is greatest when these ozone-destroying chemical elements reach a high concentration in the atmosphere. This can happen as a result of industrial processes. A prime destroyer of ozone is chlorofluorocarbon or CFC gas, which is made of carbon, chlorine, and fluorine. When CFC molecules come into contact with ultraviolet radiation, they decompose the ozone, destroying large areas of the protective ozone layer.

Nuclear explosions and rocket launches into space can also damage the ozone layer.

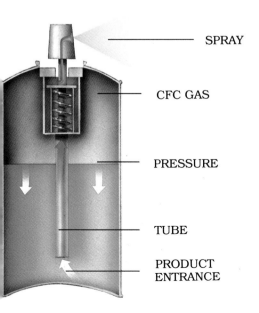

SPRAY

CFC GAS

PRESSURE

TUBE

PRODUCT ENTRANCE

◄

The disappearing ozone layer in the stratosphere is caused in part by atmospheric pollutants. One of the most damaging of these is CFC gas. CFCs are used in many everyday applications such as sprays, solvents, plastics, and air conditioning systems. There are now worldwide regulations covering the use of these substances.

The Air in Large Cities

Sources of Pollution

Pollutants are gaseous, liquid, or solid substances in the atmosphere that can cause harmful effects to both living organisms and materials, either directly or indirectly, when their concentration rises above certain levels.

Direct man-made pollution comes mainly from the combustion of fuels such as petroleum, coal, and natural gas. When these fuels are burned, gases such as carbon monoxide, benzopyrene, nitrogen oxides, and sulfur dioxide are given off.

Effects on Temperature and Climate

In cities, materials used in street paving and building construction absorb a great amount of solar radiation. In addition, rainwater, instead of being absorbed by the earth, is channeled underground. All this produces an increase in heat levels, which is why the temperature in large cities is higher than in the countryside.

The microclimate that evolves around a city contributes to the accumulation of solid, liquid, and gaseous pollutants, resulting

The growth of modern cities has brought with it major benefits but also enormous problems because city centers have been thought of more as production and consumption centers than as areas for people to live in. ▼

The factories located in the industrial belts surrounding many of today's cities give off toxic gases that eventually pollute the urban environment.

Large amounts of traffic fumes and gases poison the atmosphere.

in the familiar yellowish brown haze we
call smog.

Effects of Air Pollution on Our Health

The pollutants in the air find their way into
human beings through the respiratory
system. This system can be seriously
damaged by high concentrations of
pollutants in the air.

Pollution damages the respiratory system
by irritating the air passages in the body,
which causes an abnormal increase in
mucus production. The alteration of the
mucus and the tiny hairs located in the
trachea and the bronchi caused by
pollution make people more sensitive to
these polluting agents.

Large cities have to withstand levels of pollution that
make the local atmosphere dangerous to people's
health, especially when climatic conditions prevent
the pollution from being dispersed.

Many of the activities we carry out in large cities,
for work or recreational purposes, also cause
pollution.

Noise

Noise as Pollution

Economic growth in certain regions of the world, population increases, and crowded cities all create conditions that affect the quality of the environment.

One of these effects, which stems from the uncontrolled development of our activities in industrialized societies, has been a continual increase in noise levels.

A Noisy World

Noise is one of the factors that pollutes the air, yet it is little studied, perhaps because its harmful effects upon people's health is only noticeable over a long period of time and because noise is associated with activities that we all consider essential in modern life. This is the case, for instance, with the most common of today's noises—traffic noise in big cities.

But in any large city there are other sources of noise, such as public building and repair work, electrical transformers, air-conditioners, heating appliances, police sirens, fire trucks, ambulances, and so on. These activities are beneficial but unfortunately lead to an increase in prevailing noise levels.

Noise is an excessive and unpleasant sound that can cause discomfort. The unit used for measuring sound is the decibel (dB). 130 dB, the noise produced by a pneumatic drill, is the pain threshold for the human ear. ◄

140–1480 dB

100–140 dB

100 dB

70–80 dB

The Effects of Noise

Although we may feel that we are used to a wide variety of noises at different intensities, they nonetheless produce irritating physical and mental effects.

Loss of hearing, alterations in sleep patterns, and a state of tension called stress, are the first symptoms of the harmful effects of noise.

Our sense of hearing, which captures sound waves in the air, is designed in such a way that it can dampen certain loud sounds. However, the ear drum and the chain of small bones in the ear can be affected by continuous loud sounds. When the internal structure of the ear hardens and deteriorates, this leads to a partial loss of hearing.

There is a scale that measures the intensity of the sound produced by different sources. Sound is measured in decibels (dB). A sound level of 70 dB produces severe discomfort; even so, people often live and work in environments in which this level is exceeded.

The development of large cities means that noise is becoming increasingly important, and it is included among the group of factors that have harmful effects on our health. In this senses it should be considered as a pollutant of the environment.
▼

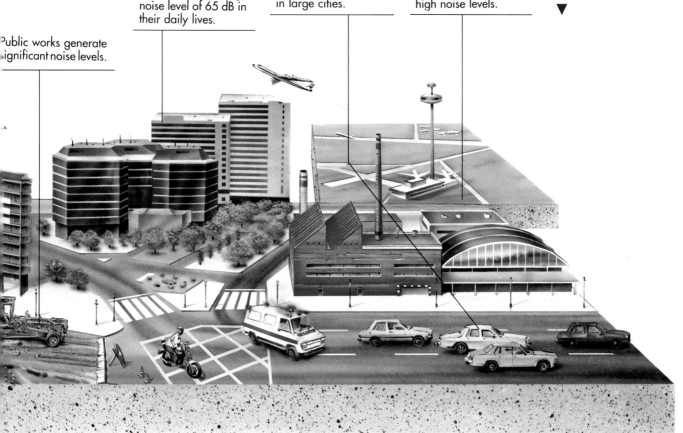

15% of the inhabitants of large cities are exposed to an average noise level of 65 dB in their daily lives.

Traffic is one of the main causes of noise in large cities.

People who live near industries located within cities or next to airports must endure high noise levels.

Public works generate significant noise levels.

Communications

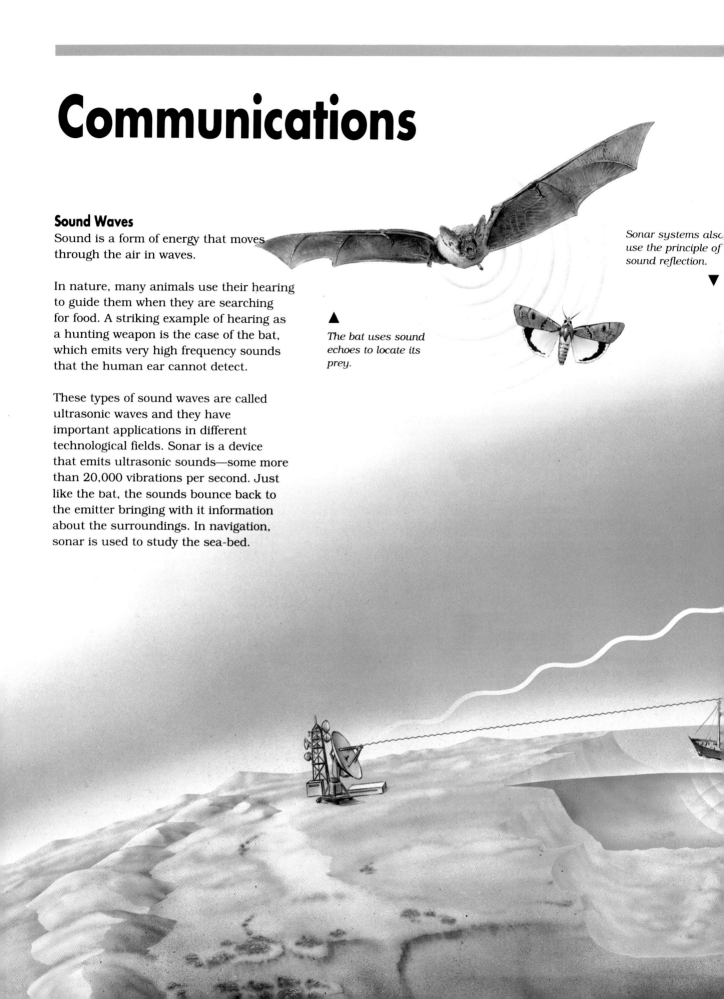

Sound Waves

Sound is a form of energy that moves through the air in waves.

In nature, many animals use their hearing to guide them when they are searching for food. A striking example of hearing as a hunting weapon is the case of the bat, which emits very high frequency sounds that the human ear cannot detect.

These types of sound waves are called ultrasonic waves and they have important applications in different technological fields. Sonar is a device that emits ultrasonic sounds—some more than 20,000 vibrations per second. Just like the bat, the sounds bounce back to the emitter bringing with it information about the surroundings. In navigation, sonar is used to study the sea-bed.

The bat uses sound echoes to locate its prey.

Sonar systems also use the principle of sound reflection.

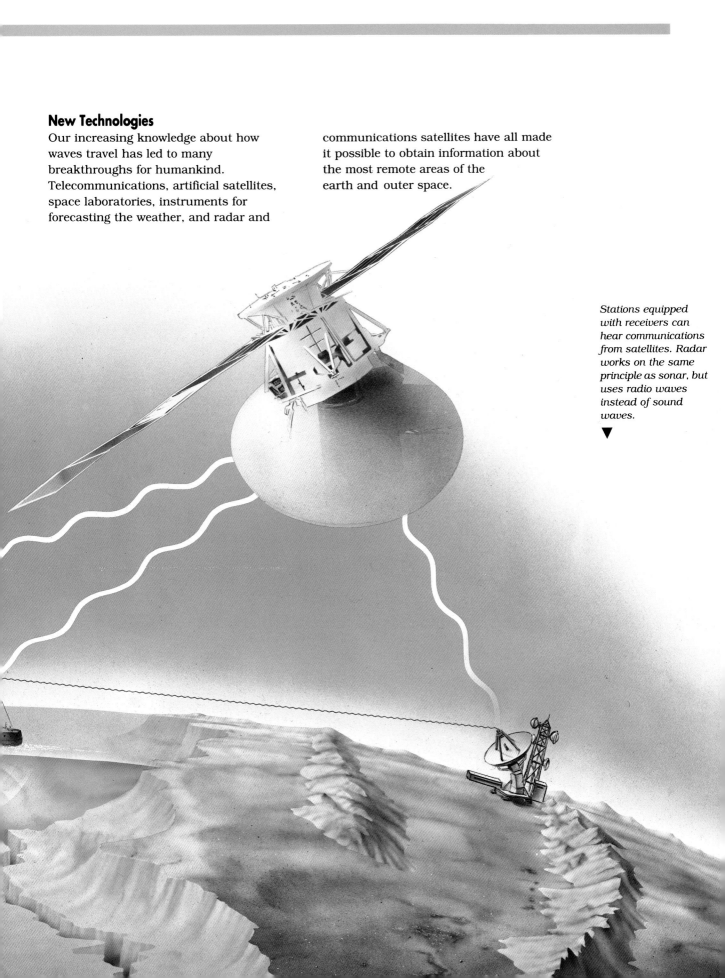

New Technologies

Our increasing knowledge about how waves travel has led to many breakthroughs for humankind. Telecommunications, artificial satellites, space laboratories, instruments for forecasting the weather, and radar and communications satellites have all made it possible to obtain information about the most remote areas of the earth and outer space.

Stations equipped with receivers can hear communications from satellites. Radar works on the same principle as sonar, but uses radio waves instead of sound waves.

▼

Activities

Oxygen is a component of the air that makes combustion possible. To prove this you can try the following experiment.

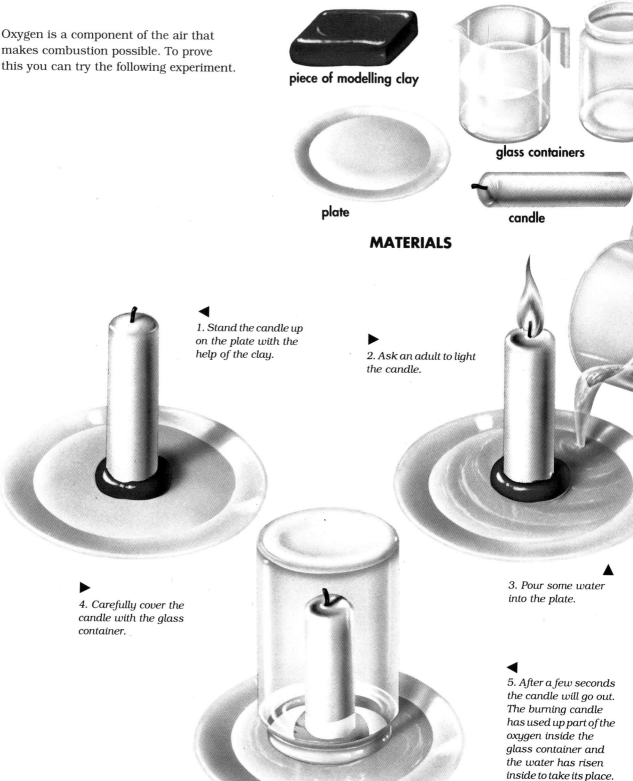

piece of modelling clay

glass containers

plate

candle

MATERIALS

◄ 1. Stand the candle up on the plate with the help of the clay.

► 2. Ask an adult to light the candle.

► 4. Carefully cover the candle with the glass container.

▲ 3. Pour some water into the plate.

◄ 5. After a few seconds the candle will go out. The burning candle has used up part of the oxygen inside the glass container and the water has risen inside to take its place.

You can prove the existence of solid particles in the air with this simple experiment.

pieces of white cardboard

plastic caps

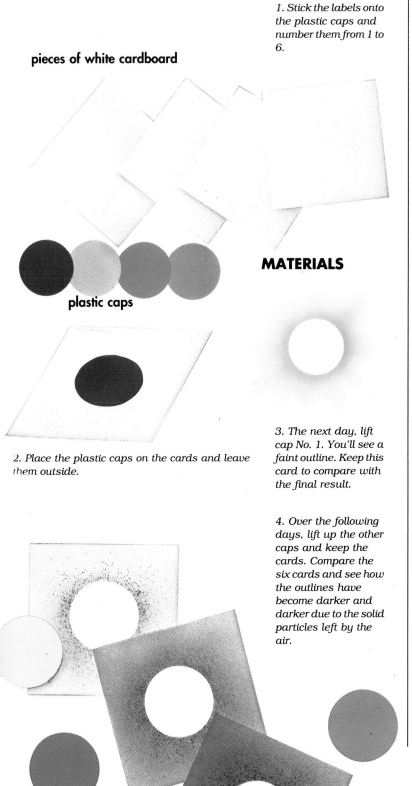

2. Place the plastic caps on the cards and leave them outside.

1. Stick the labels onto the plastic caps and number them from 1 to 6.

MATERIALS

3. The next day, lift cap No. 1. You'll see a faint outline. Keep this card to compare with the final result.

4. Over the following days, lift up the other caps and keep the cards. Compare the six cards and see how the outlines have become darker and darker due to the solid particles left by the air.

This experiment will help you to determine the acidity of rainwater. The results will be more apparent if the experiment is carried out in industrial or urban surroundings where there is a greater tendency for acid rain to be present.

glass containers

strips of litmus paper

MATERIALS

1. Put a piece of litmus paper into one of the containers full of water from the faucet.

2. Collect some rainwater in another container and put another litmus paper inside.

3. Collect more rainwater over several days and compare the

results with the previous pieces of litmus paper.

Words to Remember

CFCs Clorofluorocarbon compounds. They are artificial gaseous chemical substances that are used in many products such as aerosol sprays.

Ecosystem An integrated group of different living species that live and interact in a specific area.

Electromagnetic spectrum The range of different types of radiation. Invisible to the naked eye, the higher part of the spectrum is made up of gamma rays, X rays, and ultraviolet rays, whereas the lower range is made up of infrared rays, microwaves, and radio waves.

Fuel A mixture of hydrocarbons used in internal combustion engines. The most common fuels are oil, coal, and natural gas.

Gravity The attractive force between all material objects, including the sun, earth, and other celestial bodies.

Greenhouse effect A natural process by which the earth's atmosphere conserves its heat. Without it there would be no life on our planet.

Microorganisms An organism that can only be seen with the aid of a microscope.

Sulfur oxide A gas produced when combustible fuels such as coal and oil are burned. When it mixes with water in the atmosphere, it produces sulfuric acid, which falls to earth in the form of acid rain.

Ozone A colorless gas that is present in the atmosphere. It protects living organisms on the earth because it stops harmful ultraviolet radiation from reaching the lower parts of the atmosphere.

Photosynthesis A chemical process through which, by the action of sunlight, plants synthesize the nutrients they need from the carbon dioxide in the air.

Ultraviolet rays Invisible light from the sun that can be dangerous to living creatures in large amounts.

Index